Single Page
LIFE PLAN

Garrett K. Scanlon

ALSO BY GARRETT K. SCANLON

*Walking and Talking: 57 Stories of Success and
Humor in the Real Estate World of Business*

Single Page Life Plan for Realtors

*Lifeboard: How to Form
Your Own Personal Board of Directors*

Seeing Past Friday Night

#1 Method for Leading a
More Productive Life

Single Page
LIFE PLAN

Fast ◆ Simple ◆ Life-Changing

Garrett K. Scanlon

BALLYLONGFORD BOOKS

Ballylongford Books
2588 Welsford Road
Columbus, Ohio 43221
www.ballylongfordbooks.com

Printed and bound in the United States of America
First Printing 2013

Scanlon, Garrett K.
Single page life plan: #1 method for leading a more productive life/
Garrett K. Scanlon. — Columbus, Ohio : Ballylongford Books, c2013.

p. ; cm.

ISBN: 978-0-9753612-5-2

1. Success. 2. Goal (Psychology) 3. Self-realization. 4. Life skills.
5. Achievement motivation. 6. Well-being. 7. Stress management. I. Title.

BF637.S8 S33 2013   2013939220
        158.1—dc23   1306

Garrett K. Scanlon is available for training, consulting, and speaking. Visit www.SinglePageLifePlan.com to bring Garrett Scanlon and Single Page Life Planning to your company, group, school, or nonprofit organization.

COVER AND TEXT DESIGN BY WWW.TOTHEPOINTSOLUTIONS.COM

To
Michael and Debbie Jokovich

Contents

CONTENTS

Introduction

In Lewis Carroll's novel *Alice in Wonderland* this exchange takes place between Alice and The Cat:

Alice: Would you tell me, please, which way I ought to go from here?

The Cat: That depends a good deal on where you want to get to.

Alice: I don't care much where.

The Cat: Then it doesn't much matter which way you go.

Alice: . . . so long as I get somewhere.

The Cat: Oh, you're sure to do that, if only you walk long enough.

Few of us want to wander aimlessly through our life. But, we also do not want to be saddled with a cumbersome and complicated map.

The *Single Page Life Plan* is designed to be fast, simple and life-changing. And, the life it is designed to change is yours!

Chapter 1

The Case Against Life Plans

The case that most people make against having a life plan goes something like this:

- ○ Life plans, like business plans, are too long and complicated!

- ○ Creating a life plan requires too much time.

- ○ Why bother with a life plan when we know that outside circumstances change all the time and we will have to change course anyway?

- ○ I rarely, if ever, refer to plans I write down, so why bother?

- ○ I always try to make my life plan perfect, which is frustrating.

- ○ I fear I will not be able to live up to the goals I set.

○ A life plan will make me lose spontaneity in my life.

○ Frankly, I have just never thought about writing down a life plan and wouldn't know where to start.

Each of these points has merit! The *Single Page Life Plan* is designed to resolve all of these issues!

The *Single Page Life Plan* was created on the belief that once a life plan spills onto a second page, it gets tossed into a manila folder and is filed away until next year. They are placed out of sight and out of mind. It is true that life plans and business plans are too long and complex!

Our world seems to be getting more and more complex every day, and the new technologies that promise to save us time and energy often leave us feeling frazzled and depleted. We are bombarded by so many distractions and are pulled in so many different directions, we often wonder if we have any control over our lives!

The answer to all of this complexity is not to compound the problem with a complicated plan. Instead, we need to create a plan that simplifies our life. We need an uncomplicated plan that blows through all of the peripheries that distract us from leading better lives. We need a simple plan that focuses our attention on significant and meaningful activity. We need a *Single Page Life Plan*.

Because the *Single Page Life Plan* is simple, you will refer to it more often and it will become a fluid, modifiable plan that can withstand the inevitable changes that occur in your life.

For those who fear they will be pushed towards a rigid set of activities that will stifle spontaneity in their life, the reality is that a life plan actually *adds* spontaneity to your life.

Consider this example. Many of us feel that some of our most spontaneous activities occur when we are traveling on vacation, free of the typical constraints of everyday life. Spending time *planning* those vacation trips doesn't make us any less spontaneous. Instead, it keeps us better organized, frees up added time for us, and helps us focus our energy so that we can make the best use of our vacation time. It is the same with most aspects of life. A well-made plan actually grants you *more* flexibility to *add* spontaneity to your life.

CHAOS IS NOT YOUR FRIEND!

There is one more reason some people have for avoiding life plans. They have become comfortable with chaos!

Being comfortable with chaos manifests itself in 5 different ways.

1. **Dealing with chaos can be addicting, like a game.**

   A friend of mine once said, "Chaos is my friend!" While he was kidding, I could sense that there was a part of him that relished multitasking a hundred things at the same time. It was almost like a game for him; a game he thought he played well.

2. **Dealing with chaos begins to feel *normal*.**

   Sometimes, we become so accustomed to feeling overwhelmed by chaos, that we begin to think that it is *normal* to be that way.

3. **Accepting chaos becomes a badge of honor.**

   Some people actually wear chaos in their life as a badge of honor. It goes something like this: *Can you believe how overwhelmed my life is? My life is so scattered and hectic, I must be an important cog in this giant wheel we call life!*

4. **We equate being *busy* with being *productive*.**

   I will never forget a meeting I had, very early on in my career, with a successful owner of multifamily investment property. He asked, "How's business?"

   I replied, "Really good . . . I've never been busier?"

He bluntly asked, "Are you earning any money?"

I gave an awkward yet truthful answer, and replied, "No, not really."

Busy is not the same as *productive*.

5. Chaos provides us with a handy excuse.

How many times have you heard this? *I have so many things going on right now, there's just no way I can get it all done.* Isn't that just another way of saying, *I keep so busy how can I be expected to take care of all of those important items on my list?*

It is time to replace the insignificant activities on your schedule to make room for the important stuff!

People who focus on a specific plan are:

More thoughtful.

More intentional.

Better organized.

They are:

More productive.

More energetic.

More creative.

Chaos is sometimes unavoidable, but should never be considered inescapable. Chaos is *not* your friend!

YOUR ROAD MAP

It has been said by many others, in a variety of ways, that people who don't care where they are going, don't need a map. The rest of us, however, recognize the value of adding some direction to our lives; of setting a course that aims us towards our goals, hopes, dreams, and aspirations.

CEOs need a business plan.

Coaches need a game plan.

Builders need an architectural plan.

Pilots need a flight plan, and . . .

Leaders need a life plan!

We could go through a long list of clever quotes and famous sayings about the importance of adding focus to our life, but **the problem isn't that we don't recognize the importance of creating a plan**. The problem is that we just don't do it! But, that is about to change . . . *today*!

Today, you will create your *Single Page Life Plan*, complete with a vision statement, your chosen life-priorities at home and work, and action steps that will help you turn your dreams into reality.

The case against life plans falls apart when you reduce your plan to a single page. But as the next chapter explains, your plan must never be P.O.S.H.!

Chapter 2

Your Single Page Life Plan Is Not P.O.S.H.

The brilliance of your *Single Page Life Plan* lies in its pure simplicity. It must never be **P**erfect, **O**verloaded, **S**et-in-stone, or **H**idden.

PERFECT

Your life plan is not the *Magna Carta*! It is a document that is just as important to you, but it's different. Your life plan is a blueprint of how you want to live your life. It forces you to identify your goals and strategies, and it makes it easier to gauge results and to stay accountable. However, it is not meant to be all-inclusive or perfect.

Don't get all mired down searching for a grand epiphany here. Just get things going in the right direction.

And, make sure your plan is not . . .

OVERLOADED

Peripheries are not *Priorities*! Peripheries in your life have to earn their way to *Page One*! Until then, they are distractions; they are clutter. They are your second and third ideas that keep getting in the way of your first good idea. Place a laser focus on your most important goals. Don't let your laser beam be diffused by a wide array of useless, energy-zapping activities.

And, never let your life plan be . . .

SET IN STONE

Your plan is a *working* plan that you will want to continually update, edit, and change; sometimes in very dramatic ways. Circumstances are always changing. Like an airplane pilot, we are sure to experience cloudy days, unexpected headwinds, and high-pressure systems along our journey. We need to be nimble and to adapt quickly, as we keep our focus on our destination.

It is to be used as a tool, not adored! Be prepared to take a pen or pencil and scratch up your life plan.

Finally, for you to stay accountable to your plan, it must not be . . .

HIDDEN

Share your plan with others! Studies show that a person is more likely to achieve success while on a diet, for example, if they share their goals with friends and family. Similarly, it will be a formidable, yet positive challenge for yourself to share your life plan with others.

This will accomplish two things. First, it will motivate you to stay accountable to your goals and aspirations. Secondly, it will empower your friends, family, and colleagues to help and assist you in achieving your quest.

American Founding Father Thomas Paine once said, "A body of men holding themselves accountable to nobody, ought not be trusted by anybody." There is much to be said for being transparent to others.

If your *Single Page Life Plan* is not **perfect, overloaded, set-in-stone**, or **hidden**, you will use it! You will refer to it regularly, and utilize it to help you change course when necessary. It will be fast, simple, and life-changing!

But first, there's something you need to know about *simple . . .*

Chapter 3

Simple Is Not Easy . . . Only Better!

Don't mistake simple for easy. It takes a lot of effort and creativity to reduce things to their most simple form.

The genius of Albert Einstein was not that he could comprehend so many of the complexities of space, time, gravity, and light. Many scientists are able to do that. Instead, his genius was in his ability to simplify those complexities into an understandable theory of relativity.

He often commented that unlocking the greatest mysteries of the universe would be useless, unless you were able to make it be understandable to a young student.

Of course, Einstein did not actually *create* the simple equations that unlocked the mysteries of the universe; he *discovered* them. He discovered the *simple*. He sculpted away the clutter and left us with the meaningful. He chopped away at row upon row of mathematical calculations and left us with $E = mc^2$. He simplified complexity! It was not easy . . . only better.

That is your task. You must discover the truly meaningful things in your life; the significant things that matter. The *Single Page Life Plan* is designed to help you do that in a fast, fun, and creative way.

SYNCHRONIZE YOUR UNIVERSE!

Your life plan is not meant to be limited to certain portions or compartments of your life. Your plan needs to *synchronize* every aspect of your life towards achieving the overarching vision you have for your life. Your life does not begin and end when you walk through the doors at home, work, or house of worship; nor when you drive your car, walk that beach, or jump on that bicycle. So, get in sync!

IT'S ELEMENTAL!

There are 5 elements to your *Single Page Life Plan.*

○ Mission/Vision Statement

○ Life Categories

○ Action Steps

○ The Boxes

○ The Signature

As you can see, we're not juggling String Theory here, but we are talking about adding *energy* to your life. You could almost say that E = SPLP. Try wrapping *that* around your head, Mr. Einstein!

Let's get started!

Chapter 4

The 5 Elements of Your Life Plan

The five elements of your *Single Page Life Plan* are:

1. Mission or Vision Statement

This is the overarching vision that you have for your life. All other parts of your plan synchronize to this.

2. Life Categories

Your *Life Categories* are the 6 major highways that lead a path towards your vision statement. These *Life Categories* are what you consider to be the most vital aspects of your life.

3. Action Steps

These are the specific, achievable, and measurable steps that you commit to take on a daily basis to remain intentional, strategic, and accountable to each of your *Life Categories*.

Action Steps turn your vision into your life's reality.

4. The Boxes

There are 4 *Boxes* to your plan:

Coins are small kindnesses you can perform to help others that you encounter along your path.

Attitudes speak to the frame of mind you adopt to stay motivated in your quest.

Potholes are hurdles, and distractions in your life that steer you away from your goals.

Strengths are those character-attributes, skills, and talents you possess that can propel you towards attaining your goals.

5. Your Signature

This is the part of your *Single Page Life Plan* that will take the least amount of time, but will have the longest term of consequence. It is your *promise* to yourself that you will follow the vision you have for your future.

The Foldout Provided at the End of this Book

You will see that there is a foldout provided at the end of this book that will show you a format that incorporates these 5 elements.

Eventually, you will transfer your *Single Page Life Plan* to that foldout. When completed, you can keep it in the book to quickly and easily review it.

Makin' Copies

You might also want to make several copies of it to display at your home, office, or in front of your stationary bike or elliptical machine. Put it on the side of the refrigerator, or anywhere you are most likely to frequently reflect on your plan.

On the next page is a sample of a format used for a *Single Page Life Plan*.

My Mission Statement:
Be a positive influence in the lives of others at work & home.

FAMILY	CAREER	FINANCIAL STEWARDSHIP
Schedule weekly night out with my spouse!	Finish my continuing education requirements by June 15th	Review all of our life insurance plans & make needed changes
Prepare meals & eat together	Improve my social marketing. Join LinkedIn - Start a blog.	Reduce our debt to zero
Continually strengthen my marriage. Be a better partner!	Hire an assistant by April 20th	Create a will and a living will
Provide spiritual leadership	Increase my sales call by 20% in the first quarter of this year	Decide if we are going to have Jason or Mary be our financial planner. Stay with one person!
Be a good listener & a trusted advisor	End unproductive activities that steal time like spending too much time surfing the net	Stay true to our budget
Make a better effort to attend the kid's ballgames & events		Update our financials and improve out credit rating
Look for hobbies we can share	Network more, and attend 2 trade conferences this year	Set up a college fund for Brian
Provide financial assistance	Improve my communications skills. Join Toastmasters?	Organize all of our important financial information in 1 place
Dinner with Mom on Tuesdays	Be with positive people	Teach the kids how to save

COINS

- Thank a colleague at work today!
- Pray for someone in need
- Bake a cake for someone's birthday
- Send a stamp or a coin to a young collector
- Email an encouraging thought to a friend
- Send a box of chocolate to a friend in stress
- Order a book Online for Grandpa!

ATTITUDES

- I have an attitude of gratitude
- Carpe Diem! Seize the Day!
- I am a person who dreams heroic dreams
- The harder I work the more fortunate I am
- I am a warrior and a protector!
- I have a tolerant and inclusive attitude
- We can't change the past; only the future!

WWW.SINGLEPAGELIFEPLAN.COM

SINGLE PAGE
LIFE PLAN

FITNESS & HEALTH	TRAVEL/ENTERTAINMENT	HOBBIES & INTERESTS
Fruits, nuts, berries & veggies!	Attend a TED conference!	Take piano lessons this fall
Eat for energy and reduce salts, sugars, carbs & caffeine	Hike Yellowstone, Surf Oahu, or Safari the Serengeti	Resume my drawing/sketching
Reduce my body fat by 10%. Plan out my meals in advance.	Make use of Ben and Ann's lake-house in the spring	Take Lifelong Learning classes; Language & Cooking
Get sunlight & fresh air daily!	Plan Wimbledon for next year	Act in a local play this summer
Weight train 3 times per week, and run on the off-days	Go to the Miami Book Fair or the Sundance Film Festival!	Entertain at home every month
Begin a swimming regimen	The Smithsonian, Monticello & Arlington National Cemetery	Create a blog and resume my poetry writings
Get a physical by August 1st	Be a part of a live TV audience	Take photography classes at the university in the spring
Early to bed & early to rise!	Take a golf trip with my friends	Buy a tandem bicycle and start exploring the rails-to-trails
Use quite time and music time every day to reduce stress and to relax	Finally, see a Broadway Play!	Go camping with the Millers this year. Borrow Dan's kayak!

POTHOLES

- Surfing for hours on the Internet
- Hanging out with negative people
- Holding onto the past
- Being too sensitive to criticism from others
- Procrastination and fear of making mistakes
- Work flings and dating incompatible people
- Staying up late at night and eating past 7:00

SKILLS

- I have a good sense of humor
- I am reliable. Others can count on me
- I have good presentation & speaking skills
- I am honest and always give 100%
- I'm mechanically inclined & can fix anything
- I am well-read and stay well-informed
- I know how to coach and motivate others

Signature: _____

Chapter 5

Mission Ispossible

This is one of the shortest parts of your life plan, but might be the most difficult part to create! It is your *Mission* or *Vision Statement*. In one sense, this will set the stage for everything else in your life plan. Nothing that follows in your plan should conflict with your *Mission/Vision Statement*.

From this point on, let's refer to it as your *Vision Statement*, because it truly is going to reflect the vision you have for your future. It will reflect what *you* want your life to stand for. That's all. Wow! Seems kind of heavy, doesn't it?

But, this is where you must remember that your plan cannot be P.O.S.H. *Do not strive for perfection here.* Do your best and move on. It is a fluid and changeable document!

To reduce it to base terms, you might want to consider the silly notion that you are not going to live forever, and ask yourself this question:

If I knew that I was going to be hit by a meteor 10 years from now, how would I want to spend the next decade of my life? (By the way, it's against the rules to answer this hypothetical question by saying that you would spend the time trying to invent a device that destroys meteors!) Ask yourself, *If someone were to accurately describe that time of my life, what would I want them to be able to say about it? What would be my focus?*

Like every part of this plan, the choice at every step is yours. It is very personal and unique to you. Everyone will have a different thought as to what is their overarching purpose in life. There is no right or wrong answer, as long as it resonates with the direction you want to go.

ONE MORE THING

Your life plan is all about moving forward; it's all about the future. The past is the past, and this is about your *next* 10 years!

40 WORDS!

On the lines supplied at the end of this chapter, on page forty, write down your *Vision Statement*, in 40 words or less! Yes, that's right . . . it must be concise! Place a laser-like focus on what is truly meaningful and significant to you.

For some brainstorming help, you will find on the following pages, sample Vision Statements, listed by theme. These examples are to help you quickly generate ideas and language to form your own statement.

INSTRUCTIONS

Step 1: Circle 6 to 8 statements that most closely reflect your thoughts and feelings.

Step 2: Eliminate all but 3 of your choices.

Step 3: You can actually use these 3 choices as your *Vision Statement*, or simply use them to brainstorm ideas. Write them down in the *Work Area* on the following page, and then edit them.

Step 4: When you are satisfied with your final result, transfer it to *My Vision Statement* at the end of this chapter, on page 38.

Work Area: *Write down your final 3 choices here. Use them as your Vision Statement or to brainstorm a completely unique statement of your own! Use the work space below to edit your words and then transfer your final Vision Statement to page 38.*

_____

_____

_____

SAMPLE VISION STATEMENTS

General:

Live each day as if it were my last; Carpe Diem!

Live a simple and content life.

Seek fame and fortune and my place in the world.

Be a good student, teacher, apprentice, and mentor.

Leave a significant mark on the world.

Live up to my potential in life.

Maintain an attitude of gratitude.

Never settle.

Be healthy, wealthy, and wise.

Be intentional as I continue my path to a new career and life.

Laugh, smile, love, advocate, exercise, work, learn, and teach.

Nature:

Continually learn about my place in the world and make the world a better place.

Continually improve my heart, mind, soul, and body through truth, love, and discipline.

Live in union with nature and enjoy my life.

Be in community with my local surroundings, the earth, the universe, and others.

Enjoy the journey of life.

Be peaceful and content by discovering laughter, love, and happiness.

Use my personal strengths to make the world a better place.

Continued on next page…

God:

Make the most of the skills, talents, and abilities God gave me to lead a significant life.

Put God first in my life, and lead my life according to the plan God has for me.

Show love and give love through faith, hope, and caring.

Continually seek God's plan for my life and have the courage to act on that wisdom.

Worship God with all my heart, mind, and strength.

Reflect God's love in everything I do, and strive to do.

Love and honor God and serve others.

Continually improve my relationship with God, my family, friends, and colleagues.

Be grateful for my blessings and share them with others.

Do unto others as I would have them do unto me.

Be spiritually, mentally, and physically healthy.

Service:

Enjoy all that life has to offer and give back to others.

Love, protect, and defend those around me.

Help others every day and be a joy to others.

Change the world by being a positive force for others.

Be a protector, giver, provider, and advisor to others to help them reach their potential.

Bring happiness to people everywhere to the best of my ability.

Make a positive difference in the lives of others and enjoy the ride!

Leadership:

Lead by example by continually striving to become a better person.

Be a leader of my family, my friends, and my colleagues.

Be an encourager to others.

Lead by example.

Be passionate, enthusiastic, and encouraging to others.

Generously share my time and talents with family and friends.

Be a good wife, mother, daughter, sister, aunt, grandparent, mentor and coach.

Be a good husband, father, son, brother, uncle, grandparent, mentor and coach.

Be a good influence on my family, colleagues, teammates, and friends.

Love and Health:

Love life and live life to the fullest.

Learn to love my life and to accept my life completely.

Be true to myself, love others, and enjoy life.

Love and be loved in return.

Strive to be healthy in mind, body, and spirit.

Have a healthy heart, mind, and soul.

Have a healthy marriage, healthy family, and healthy relationships.

Laugh, love, and make people smile.

SINGLE PAGE LIFE PLAN

My Vision Statement

_____

_____

_____

_____

_____

_____

_____

_____

_____

_____

_____

_____

_____

_____

_____

_____

_____

_____

Congratulations! The heavy lifting is done. You have just completed what many people consider to be the most difficult part of creating your life plan. It often takes the longest amount of time. Remember though, your goal is not to reach perfection here.

Chapter 6

Categorically Speaking

One day when I was a kid, my older brother was in our backyard, holding a magnifying glass very steadily over a dry leaf. I watched as the leaf started to smoke. Soon, the leaf began to ignite.

"Whoa . . . what was *that*!?" I asked.

My brother explained how the magnifying glass focused all of the sun's energy that was going through the glass, onto the leaf, which created a tremendous amount of heat.

"Here, let me show you," he said, as he focused it on my hand.

Yes, I fell for it.

No, I will never forget that lesson.

But I will also never forget looking up to the sky with both wonder and awe, at how powerful that sun must be if you could actually ignite something simply by focusing just a little bit of its energy, using a $2 magnifying glass!

Today, you are going to be the magnifying glass.

Following are 24 different *Life Categories* for you to choose from. Look upon them as you would the entire light spectrum in the sky. It is up to you to funnel these various categories down to the 6 most important aspects of your life. Focus *your* energy on those things that are truly significant.

If you have other, more important *Life Categories* in your life that are not listed here, choose yours! This is *your* life plan. The following examples exist only to serve as an aid for you to streamline your thoughts.

So, let's go!

Step 1: Circle 8 to 10 statements that most closely reflect your thoughts and feelings.

Step 2: Eliminate all but 6 of those.

LIFE CATEGORIES

LIFE CATEGORIES

Fill in your chosen 6 Life Categories along with their corresponding page numbers:

1st Life Category   Page #

2nd Life Category   Page #

3rd Life Category   Page #

4th Life Category   Page #

5th Life Category   Page #

6th Life Category   Page #

You are starting to get the picture! Let's take a look!

In terms of time, your plan is about 40% complete:

SINGLE PAGE LIFE PLAN

You created a *Vision Statement*: _____

_____

_____

You chose 6 *Life Categories*:

Next, you will blaze a trail of *Action Steps:*

Boxes	Boxes	Boxes	Boxes

Signature _____

Chapter 7

Action Steps Must *Earn* Their Way to Page One

Action Steps are the heart and soul of your life plan. They must be *Sammy*:

- o **S**pecific
- o **A**chievable
- o **M**easureable

Your *Action Steps* force you to be:

- o **S**trategic in how you accomplish your goals.
- o **A**ccountable to the plan you create for your life.
- o **M**ethodical and intentional with your time.

Your action steps must *earn* their way to page one!

THE POWER OF A SINGLE ACTION STEP!

One Example: If you could add an hour to every week of your life, how would you spend those 52 extra hours that you pick up every year? Exercising? Reading? Enjoying some quiet time?

If you choose as one of your *Action Steps, Stop Hitting the Snooze Button!* you will gain those 52 extra hours because most snooze alarms are set for 9 minutes; times 7 days, is an hour per week!

This illustrates the power of a single *Action Step*. A time management consultant once told me that some doctors often run 15 minutes behind schedule all day long, for the simple reason that they begin their first appointment of the day, with their very first patient, 15 minutes late! Avoiding the snooze button might help alleviate 9 minutes of that.

Another Example: Seven years ago, on January 1st, I decided to do a simple thing . . . I decided to drink water instead of ordering soft drinks in a restaurant. Since then, I have replaced over 200 gallons of caramel colored, caffeinated pop with clear water, and have saved over $3,500 in after tax dollars along the way. This shows the power of a seemingly innocuous, relatively small *Action Step* (after 10 days I actually preferred the taste of the water). *Action Steps*, large and small, can be life-changing!

HOW TO SYNCHRONIZE ACTION STEPS!

Every *Action Step* you choose must be in concert with your *Vision Statement* and your *Life Categories*.

For instance, one of your categories might be *Hobbies and Interests*. Under that category, let's say you pick *Golf* as one of your legitimate passions in life. You designate it as an *Action Step* in your life.

But, perhaps you also recognize that it can be a very time-consuming activity. You might feel concerned that it will compete too much against the *Action Steps* of your other categories, such as *Friends*, or *Health and Fitness*.

So, instead of just grabbing your golf bag, heading out to the golf course on a whim, and paying for a cart, maybe you could schedule a tee time with some past classmates and *walk* the course. It would now dovetail with your other *Action Steps* to *get together with old friends*, *lift weights*, and *aerobically exercise*.

By becoming more intentional in your activity, you will lead a more productive life that is in-sync with all of your goals.

FROM PLANNING TO DOING!

The best plan in the world is worthless if it doesn't result in measurable action. Knowledge, ideas and good intentions are useless without implementation.

Action Steps perform 2 functions:

1. They take up space!

As you fill your day with positive, purposeful *Action Steps*, there is less room for the inconsequential, superfluous, and the peripheral.

2. They become habits of behavior.

As you implement them on a consistent basis, your *Action Steps* become habits that will literally transform your life as you begin acting in accordance with your real intent!

This chapter provides you with a list of *Action Steps* that relate to each one of your *Life Categories*. These lists will help you brainstorm ideas so that you can more easily determine *Action Steps* that resonate with you.

Challenge yourself by writing down *Action Steps* that are **specific**, **achievable**, and **measureable** . . .

TARGET DATES AND TIME DEADLINES

Attach target dates to your action steps when applicable. For instance:

Begin swimming regimen by April 1.
is better than
Exercise more often.

No snacks after 7 pm!
is better than
Eat less junk food.

INSTRUCTIONS:

Step 1: Write down the page numbers that are next to the *Life Categories* that you chose on page 41:

_____ _____ _____ _____ _____ _____

Step 2: Go to each one of those pages in this book and circle between 10 and 12 *Action Steps*.

Step 3: Eliminate all but 6 to 8 of those *Action Steps*, by crossing them out.

After you have picked 6 to 8 action steps for each of your *Life Categories*, proceed to Chapter 8: *Filling Boxes*.

24 Life Categories

and Their

Corresponding

Action Steps

Action Steps for . . .

Advocacy

GETTING STARTED:
- Educate myself about advocacy
- Join advocacy groups
- Join a lobbying firm
- Volunteer for a campaign
- Join a support group
- Take classes related to a field of advocacy
- Find like-minded individuals
- Find an honorable cause I believe in!
- Develop coalitions
- Research groups
- Get an advocate job
- Get fundraiser job

CHOOSE WHICH TYPE OF ADVOCACY:
- Animal rights
- Climate change
- Youth advocacy
- Drug & alcohol
- Religious
- Second Amendment
- Small-group advocacy
- Large-group mass advocacy
- Ideological & legislative
- Media advocacy
- Civil Rights
- Legal and Political
- Environmental
- Health advocacy

EXPRESS MYSELF:
- Begin a blog
- Begin a website
- Write a book
- Write articles
- Letters to the editor!
- Start small advocacy groups
- Become a counselor

*Write down 6 to 8 of your Action Steps for **Advocacy:***

_____

_____

_____

_____

_____

_____

_____

_____

_____

_____

_____

_____

_____

_____

Action Steps for . . .

Artistic & Creative

TEACHING AND LEARNING:
- Take a college class
- Take cooking classes
- Study new languages
- Create a rock garden!
- Teach a class
- Read how-to books
- Attend conventions
- Take a photography class
- Read more
- Learn to draw and write cartoons
- Take lifelong learning classes
- Take acting classes
- Tutor other people
- Prepare and give a lecture
- Create a website
- Create a blog
- Learn piano

MAKING THINGS:
- Do more gardening
- Do sculpting
- Make jewelry
- Start sewing/knitting
- Make furniture
- Flower-arranging
- Cook for someone
- Start a new business
- Begin painting!
- Make a memory jar
- Draw, paint, sketch!

OTHER:
- Go to the theatre
- Go to more concerts
- Go to the symphony
- Entertain at home
- Join a book club
- Film a movie
- Dye my hair
- Change my wardrobe
- Act in a local play

WRITING AND SINGING:
- Write poetry
- Write songs
- Begin a novel
- Take a voice lesson
- Sing in a choir
- Send cards & letters
- Write my biography

- Write a journal
- Sing Karaoke
- Write haiku
- Take dance lessons
- Take up an instrument
- Create music
- Write a guest blog

*List your Action Steps for **Artistic and Creative:***

_____

_____

_____

_____

_____

_____

_____

_____

_____

Action Steps for . . .

Battle Illness

Doctors and Nurses:

- Be prepared for meetings with doctors & nurses
- Prepare questions for all doctor meetings
- Actively participate in my care!
- Ask questions, and get answers
- Get that 2nd opinion!
- Record any adverse effects of medicines
- Keep written record of all symptoms
- Meet with a therapist
- Take my meds timely
- Keep a healthy diet!
- Research new advances
- Continually educate myself
- Knowledge is Power!

Engage Others:

- Battle illnesses *as a family*!
- Enlist the help of others
- Join support groups

- Express my feelings to others
- Help others deal with this challenge
- Keep things in perspective
- Put other's concerns above mine
- Be surrounded by positive people
- Confide in my spiritual advisor
- Confide in those I trust

Attitude & Spiritual Strengths:

- Appreciate your body's capability—accept its limitations
- Appreciate my strengths and adapt to my weaknesses
- Do not fear feelings of confusion, worry, or vulnerability
- Know worry and sadness are natural
- Recognize my emotions when they surface
- Laugh more

- Be understanding of other's reaction to the illness
- Stay strong emotionally, mentally, physically, and spiritually
- Read positive material
- Remember that God made us all unique for a reason
- *Offer up* suffering
- Be a warrior!
- Accept that the grieving process is natural
- Be grateful for every blessing
- Be patient, strong, and persistent
- Experience joy when joy appears
- Leave no room for anger
- Look to God for Grace
- My strength comes from God
- Pray for courage
- Trust in prayer
- Remember we are not alone

List your 6 to 8 Action Steps for **Battle Illness:**

_____

_____

_____

_____

_____

_____

_____

_____

Action Steps for . . .

Career

EDUCATION:
- Attend seminars
- Complete contin. ed.
- Complete my MBA
- Join in on webinars
- Learn Excel
- Learn PowerPoint
- Learn Photoshop
- Learn WordPress
- Obtain added certifications
- Read books & articles
- Learn new skills

TIME MANAGEMENT:
- Take time to brainstorm
- Review my plan weekly & monthly
- End unproductive activities
- Organize my work space!
- Work smarter, not harder
- Reduce distractions
- Remember to be punctual
- Give my goals deadlines

- Delegate better
- Improve filing system
- Carry a spiral notebook!

LEADERSHIP:
- Be an encourager
- Be a teacher!
- Help others achieve their goals
- Lead by example
- Seek increased responsibility
- Participate on committees

PERSONAL GROWTH:
- Seek mentors
- Join a mastermind group
- Join the Rotary Club and/or Chamber of Commerce
- Join Toastmasters
- Sign up for coaching programs
- Be surrounded by talented people
- Become an expert
- Form a personal lifeboard

BRANDING AND SOCIAL MARKETING:

- Enhance company brand & reputation
- Improve social media marketing
- Update my LinkedIn profile
- Tweet!
- Add a Facebook business page
- Begin a web-blog
- Update my webpage

OTHER:

- Focus on customer satisfaction

- Be a problem solver
- Set a business plan
- Strategize for growth
- Focus on my projects
- Innovate and create!
- Increase my sales efforts
- Give and attract more referrals
- Improve networking
- Take responsibility!
- Improve my public speaking
- Seek out apprentices
- Hire an assistant
- Improve my communication skills

List your Action Steps for **Career:**

_____

_____

_____

_____

_____

_____

_____

Action Steps for . . .

College Search

RESEARCH:

- Research Admission requirements
- Visit colleges and universities
- Research the various colleges online
- Enroll in a class on finding colleges
- Learn about grants and scholarships
- Follow the research— not the friends!
- See school counselor

FINANCING AND BUDGETS:

- Set a budget
- Take PSAT as a sophomore
- Take SAT and ACT
- Compare all tuition costs
- Government forms!
- Research available financial aid
- Keep it affordable!
- Avoid unmanageable debt at all times!

PREPARATION:

- Determine our school criteria
- Take college summer program
- Set up college interviews
- Meet with guidance counselors
- Apply early!
- File for *early decision*
- Have backup schools in mind
- Determine the major first!
- Take virtual tours
- Make sure to get good grades and to graduate from high school!

*List your Action Steps for **College Search:***

_____

_____

_____

_____

_____

_____

_____

_____

_____

_____

_____

_____

Action Steps for ...

Faith and Prayer

- Attend church regularly
- Join a Bible study
- Seek out truth
- Begin and end each day with prayer
- Pray for others
- Keep God #1 in my life
- Be a spiritual leader
- Lead spiritually by example!
- Pick out a house of worship
- Enroll in classes
- Seek better understanding
- Seek spiritual guidance
- Mentor those who need help
- Remember to tithe!
- Create a prayer list
- Pray continually for our marriage
- Pray for our future in-laws
- Pray for family and friends
- Pray for our country
- Read the Good Book daily!
- Stay involved at my house of worship
- Be reflective
- Set aside quiet time each day
- Fast with intention
- Leadership begins at home!

*List your 6 to 8 Action Steps for **Faith and Prayer:***

Faith & Prayer

_____

_____

_____

_____

_____

_____

_____

_____

_____

_____

_____

_____

Action Steps for . . .

Family

- Schedule regular meetings with

  _____

- Schedule regular meetings with

  _____

- Visit sick or homebound relatives
- Pray together as a family
- Have long 1-on-1 talks
- Share hobbies together
- Prepare meals together
- Love unconditionally!
- Play board games together
- Be a good listener and trusted advisor
- Explore music together
- Plan joint projects
- Help them with their life plans
- Teach them skills and independence!
- Help kids with their homework
- Help out financially
- Plan family vacations together
- Be more intentional regarding family relationships
- Go to the kid's games and activities
- Do estate planning
- Have *date night* with my spouse!
- Continually strengthen our marriage
- Schedule time with extended family members
- Attend events of nieces & nephews
- Be a better partner in life
- Provide spiritual leadership!
- Begin and continue family traditions
- Listen to their dreams and thoughts
- Help oversee health issues
- Create wills, trusts, and insurance policies
- Become involved with school activities
- Be an encourager!

*List your 6 to 8 Action Steps for **Family:***

_____

_____ **Family**

_____

_____

_____

_____

_____

_____

_____

_____

_____

_____

_____

_____

Action Steps for . . .

Financial Stewardship

INSURANCE:
- Be properly insured!
- Car
- Disability
- Health
- House
- Life

CREDIT AND DEBT:
- Maintain good credit
- Pay all bills on time
- Credit card mgt.
- Cut up credit cards!
- Live within our means
- Manage and reduce debt
- Reduce debt to zero
- Stay true to our budget
- Update the financials
- Pay taxes on time
- Use the *envelope method* for our bills

SAVINGS AND FUNDS:
- Do estate planning
- Rainy day fund
- Consult a talented financial planner
- Establish a savings account
- Maximize SEP Acct.
- Set up school and college funds

OTHER:
- Write a living will
- Write a regular will
- Help kids with their finances
- Keep four years of tax returns
- House & car maintenance plans
- Organize important documents
- Set financial goals and plans!

*List your Action Steps for **Financial Stewardship:***

_____

_____

_____ **Financial Stewardship**

_____

_____

_____

_____

_____

_____

_____

_____

_____

_____

_____

Action Steps for . . .

Fitness & Health

HEALTH:
- Annual doctor checkups
- Increase my stamina!
- Lower my cholesterol
- Don't hit the snooze button—get up!
- Early to bed/Early to rise
- Get fresh air and sunlight each day
- Obtain proper weight
- Quit bad habits
- Set good example for the kids
- Purchase a new bed
- Reduce body fat 10%!
- Improve my flexibility
- Use quiet time-music time to reduce stress

- Take vitamins
- Take cooking classes
- Kick the caffeine!
- Overcome emotional eating
- Plan out my meals in advance
- Stay hydrated
- Subscribe to fitness journals

EXERCISE ACTIVITIES:
- Biking
- Dancing
- Dog walking
- Kayaking
- Take the stairs!
- Swimming
- Self-defense

DIET:
- Eat nuts, berries, fruits, vegetables
- Eat for energy
- Reduce salts and sugars
- Eat and drink healthier
- Eliminate soft drinks

FITNESS EXERCISING:
- Aerobic training
- Bodybuilding
- Bolster strength 10%
- X train with weights
- Exercise with consistency

- Exercise my mind
- Hiking
- Jogging
- Horseback riding
- Overall fitness plan!

- Pilates
- Running
- Walk 15 mins/day
- Workout 3x weekly
- Yoga

List your 6 to 8 Action Steps for **Fitness & Health:**

_____

_____

_____

_____

_____

_____

_____

_____

Action Steps for . . .

Friends

- Stay in touch
- Write 2 letters every month
- Plan calls in advance
- Remember my friends' birthdays
- Connect on Facebook
- Visit them *where they are*
- Think how I can help with their challenges
- Set up a Skype account
- Plan short trips together
- Always be loyal
- Send updated family photos
- Send a Hallmark card
- Ask about their families
- Plan group outings
- Plan a vacation together
- Schedule rounds of golf
- Organize a new book club
- Schedule quarterly group get-togethers
- Always be helpful
- Avoid political discussions
- Focus on our commonalities
- Become a better listener and do not judge

*List your 6 to 8 Action Steps for **Friends:***

_____

_____

_____

_____

Friends

_____

_____

_____

_____

_____

_____

_____

Action Steps for . . .

Grandparenting

LISTEN AND ENCOURAGE:

- Ask about their challenges
- Be Facebook friends
- Be a trusted advisor
- Be a good listener & encourager
- Be Skype friends
- Listen to their dreams and thoughts
- Meet for breakfast or lunch
- Spend one-on-one time together
- Volunteer at their school
- Help them with their life plan
- Schedule *Grandkid Day*
- Schedule special days

SHARED ACTIVITIES AND INTERESTS:

- Board games and card games
- Take a cooking class together
- Engage in shared hobbies
- Explore music and art together
- Exercise together
- Go to their events
- Read together
- Plan joint projects
- Prepare meals with each other
- Play internet games
- Visit place of worship together
- Visit the zoo!
- Work in the yard & garden together

TRAVEL ACTIVITIES:

- Family vacation together
- Fish/Camp/Explore together
- Outdoor adventuring
- Plan mini-road trips
- Visit theme parks
- Visit museums
- Visit historical sites

TEACHING AND SHARING:

- Discuss life lessons
- Help with their schoolwork
- Share family values
- Share family history
- Teach them skills
- Tell them a story from my youth
- Warn them of drugs and alcohol
- Write a diary for them

OTHER:

- Consider updating my will
- Letters, cards, & souvenirs!
- Pray for my grandchildren
- Schedule family reunions
- Start a savings account
- Start/extend family traditions

Grandparenting

On the next page list Grandparenting *Action Steps . . .*

List your 6 to 8 Action Steps for **Grandparenting:**

_____

_____

_____

_____

_____

_____

_____

_____

_____

_____

_____

_____

Action Steps for . . .

Hobbies & Interests

ADVENTURES AND TRAVEL:
- Day trips!
- Plan a major trip every year
- Spelunking
- Visit the country of my ancestors
- Visit historical sites
- Visit museums
- Visit parks

COLLECTING:
- Books
- Coins
- Rocks or shells
- Souvenirs
- Stamps

COOKING:
- Bread making
- Cake decorating
- Canning
- Preserving fruit
- Recipe-writing and sharing

CRAFTING:
- Candle making
- Cross stitching
- Crocheting
- Embroidery
- Floral arranging
- Handcrafting
- Jewelry
- Leather-crafting
- Macramé
- Origami
- Paper crafts
- Preserving flowers
- Quilting
- Sewing
- Stain-glassing
- Weaving
- Woodworking

MUSIC:
- Saxophone
- Piano
- Violin
- Singing lessons
- Songwriting

GAMES:
- Chess
- Crosswords
- Mahjong
- Playing bridge
- Playing backgammon
- Playing cards
- Board games
- Video games
- Puzzles
- Scrabble
- Sudoku

WATER ACTIVITIES:
- Boating & canoeing
- Fishing
- River rafting
- Go Sailing!
- Scuba diving
- Snorkeling

OUTDOORS:
- Camping
- Gardening
- Flying Kites
- Hiking
- Skiing
- Surfing

OTHER:
- Book Club
- Carpentry
- Chopping wood
- Coaching
- Dancing
- Debating
- Drawing & Sketching
- Entertaining
- Genealogy
- Journaling
- Language classes
- Model trains
- Model Airplane flying
- Painting
- Photography
- Reading
- Restoring furniture
- Scrapbooking
- Sculpting
- Shopping
- Twitter
- Volunteer
- Watching movies
- Woodcarving
- Wine making
- Wine tasting
- Writing

List your 6 to 8 Action Steps for **Hobbies and Interests:**

_____

_____

_____

_____

_____

_____ **Hobbies**

_____

_____

_____

_____

_____

_____

Action Steps for . . .

Home Environment

DECORATING AND MUSIC:

- Make visually pleasing & inviting
- Make surroundings comfortable
- Get a home decorator
- Add fresh flowers!
- Paint with new colors
- Update furnishings
- New floor coverings
- Add a sound system

CREATING SPACES AND PLACES:

- Have an orderly environment for kids
- Create learning areas
- Quite reading areas
- Area for family meals and family games
- An area for reflection
- Finish the basement!
- A room for exercise
- Family archives place
- A room for our guests

POLICIES:

- Policies for computer, phone, TV & music

MAINTENANCE AND UPKEEP:

- Repairs & upkeep list
- Cleaning schedules
- Fall-Winter cleaning
- Interior maint. list
- Exterior maint. list
- Divide house duties
- Review home safety issues
- Organize our home, room by room
- When it doubt, throw it out!
- Have utility company perform house energy audit!
- Make our home eco-friendly!
- Check batteries and furnace filters!

*List your 6 to 8 Action Steps for **Home Environment:***

_____

_____

_____

_____

_____

_____ **Home**

_____

_____

_____

_____

_____

_____

Action Steps for . . .

Job Search

RESUMES AND INTERVIEWS:
- Update my resume
- Create a strong cover letter
- Post resumes on web
- Update my references
- Update Facebook and LinkedIn profile
- Obtain new referrals
- Get testimonials
- Create *elevator pitch*
- Take the civil service exam
- Prepare for interview
- Practice interview questions

ASKING FOR HELP:
- Hire search experts
- Ask friends and family for leads
- Ask teachers and colleagues for leads
- Use campus career centers
- Leverage my internship
- Tweet/Post/Email!
- Network!

IDEAS AND STRATEGIES:
- Target-list companies
- Google job-alerts
- Keep getting up early every day!
- Answer local ads
- Personally visit companies
- Door-knock & cold-call, & send letters
- Go thru Yellow Pages
- Attend a jobs fair!
- Join professional and alumni groups
- twitterjobsearch.com
- indeed.com
- naceweb.com
- simplyhired.com
- theLadders.com
- Stay persistent & positive!!

*List your 6 to 8 Action Steps for **Job Search:***

_____

_____

_____

_____

_____

_____

_____

_____

_____

_____

_____

_____

Action Steps for ...

Laughter

READ, LEARN AND WATCH:

- Learn a new joke every day
- Read a hilarious book
- Watch more comedies
- Read the comic page every day
- Go to live comedy shows
- Read a book by Erma Bombeck
- Become a student of humor
- Study great humorists
- Watch the Comedy Channel
- Look for hilarity in life

ADD TO THE LAUGHTER:

- Help make others laugh
- Take time to find the funny side of life
- Be positive
- Lighten up! Don't be so serious
- Film a funny movie
- Add laughter & joy to my life
- Film a humorous podcast
- Smile more often!
- Try stand-up comedy
- Laugh with my friends
- Contribute funny things to blogs
- Record and publish a humor CD

*List your 6 to 8 Action Steps for **Laughter:***

_____

_____

_____

_____

_____

_____

Laughter

_____

_____

_____

_____

_____

Action Steps for . . .

Learning

- Continuing education classes
- Be selective in my reading
- Take music lessons
- Attend adult classes
- Take up a new sport
- Learn a completely new activity
- Take a self-defense class
- Learn to perform CPR
- Take new and different routes to work
- Visit small towns on weekends
- Rediscover my local library!
- Read one biography every month
- Take a comedy class
- Learn to play chess
- Take a Lifelong Learning class

- Visit historical and art museums
- Go on educational cruises
- Take health and wellness programs
- Attend writing conferences
- Travel to book festivals
- Take computer classes
- Sign up for online webinars
- Join local book clubs
- Learn how to dance!
- Increase my travels abroad!
- Get an added degree or an accreditation
- Go to Shakespearean festivals
- Learn a new language!

*List your 6 to 8 Action Steps for **Learning:***

_____

_____

_____

_____

_____

_____

_____

Learning

_____

_____

_____

_____

_____

Action Steps for . . .

Organization

- Streamline the bills
- Pay my bills online
- All insurance policies in one place!
- All passwords in one place!
- Organize the house
- Organize my wallet, purse, or briefcase
- Read books on organizing
- Hire an organizational expert
- Create a better filing system
- Create a filing system for my emails
- Bookmark my top 30 websites
- Create one password list!
- Car records, title, and insurance
- Notes and Mortgages
- Banking activity
- Organize medical records
- Wills and Trusts
- Intellectual property
- Simplify my life!
- Reduce paperwork
- Unclutter my world
- Get rid of all the *stuff*!
- Purchase new contact software
- Back up computer files on a separate drive
- Touch paper once!

List your 6 to 8 Action Steps for **Organization:**

_____

_____

_____

_____

_____

_____

_____

_____ **Organization**

_____

_____

_____

_____

Action Steps for . . .

Parenting

FAMILY TIME:
- Plan vacations regularly
- Rediscover the museums/libraries
- Attend more of the kid's activities
- Pray with them
- Read with them
- Talk with the kids every day
- Prepare meals together
- Worship together
- Spend one-on-one time together
- Coach one of their sports teams
- Plan mini-road trips
- Visit zoos and parks
- Explore music & art together
- Outdoor-adventure together
- Volunteer at their school

TEACHING AND ENCOURAGEMENT:
- Provide spiritual leadership
- Discuss life lessons
- Add educational direction
- Help with goal planning
- Oversee their health issues
- Help them build self-confidence
- Be an encourager
- Teach about dangers of drugs and alcohol
- Encourage physical fitness
- Help them form a life plan
- Help with homework and lesson plans
- Be a trusted advisor to the children

FINANCIAL:
- Coach the kids on financial planning
- Help them create savings accounts
- Update our life insurance policies
- Set up educational funds
- Set up Wills & Trusts

OTHER:
- Give loving discipline
- Pray for the kids
- Have shared hobbies
- Laugh together!

- Start various family traditions
- Be a trusted advisor
- Write a diary for kids for when they're older

List your 6 to 8 Action Steps for **Parenting:**

_____

_____

_____

_____

_____

_____

_____

Parenting

_____

_____

_____

_____

Action Steps for . . .

Sports & Athletics

- Airplane flying
- Archery
- Baseball
- Basketball
- Biking
- Biathlon
- Billiards
- Boating
- Bowling
- Boxing
- Broomball
- Canoeing
- Car racing
- Cheerleading
- Croquet
- Cricket
- Crew
- Dancing
- Diving
- Dirt biking
- Darts
- Fencing
- Fishing
- Hiking
- Hunting
- Motorcycle racing
- Paralympics

- Polo
- Rodeo
- Racquetball
- Rollerblading
- Rowing
- Rugby
- Shooting—skeet, target, and trap
- Skateboarding
- Skiing-snow, water, and cross-country
- Snowboarding
- Soccer
- Softball
- Skating
- Steeplechase
- Surfing
- Table tennis
- Tae Kwan Do
- Tennis
- Track and Field
- Volleyball—beach
- Volleyball—Indoor
- Water Polo
- Weightlifting
- Wheelchair sports
- Wrestling

*List your 6 to 8 Action Steps for **Sports & Athletics:***

_____

_____

_____

_____

_____

_____

_____

_____

_____

Sports

_____

_____

_____

Action Steps for . . .

Social Media

OVERALL PLANNING:

- Develop objectives & goals
- Buy upgraded computer
- Create an overall PR plan
- Identify my ideal contacts
- Identify my audience
- Choose who to connect with
- Form Email lists
- Create web fame
- E-learning campaign
- Hire a consultant
- Increase my SEO
- Sell my books on Amazon and B&N
- Create a social media schedule
- Attract followers with free stuff!
- Promote webinars

DEVELOP CONTENT:

- Create an editorial calendar
- Create e-books
- Post more content
- Write free newsletters
- Create an online radio show
- Create an iTunes book CD
- Create great content!
- Start a blog!
- Make YouTube videos & podcasts
- Find a freelancer
- Write guest blog posts
- Write online articles
- Publish on EzineArticles.com
- Publish polls on my blog
- Create a book from my blog posts

CREATE SITES AND PAGES:
- Facebook profile
- FB business page
- LinkedIn profile
- LinkedIn group
- My business website
- My personal website
- Open MySpace Acct
- Close MySpace Acct
- Develop Web TV site
- Make Amazon profile
- Use WordPress or BlogSpot for blog
- Set up Twitter Acct

SHARE!
- Podcast at the site, Blubrry.com
- Upload to SlideShare
- Push images to Flickr
- Feed posts to Twitter
- Upload video content to TubeMogul
- Bookmark Digg, Ning StumbleUpon, Reddit

- Picasa web albums
- Make use of Tumblr
- Publish reviews

OTHER:
- Improve my email signature
- Set Google alerts
- Learn proper online etiquette
- Learn to use GoToMeeting.com
- Host talk show at BlogTalkRadio.com
- Create a YouTube Channel
- Learn online legal issues regarding use
- Squidoo and Yelp
- Hold virtual conferences
- Learn sequence marketing
- Add E-commerce to my website

Social Media

On the next page list your Action Steps for Social Media. . .

*List your Action Steps for **Social Media:***

_____

_____

_____

_____

_____

_____

_____

_____

_____

_____

_____

_____

Action Steps for . . .

Travel and Entertainment

**SPECIFIC EVENTS
AND SHOWS:**
- The Kentucky Derby!
- The Daytona 500
- Mardi Gras
- Cirque du Soliel!
- A TED Conference
- Shakespeare Festival
- The Miami Book Fair
- CMA Music Festival
- Carnival!
- U.S. Open tickets!
- Germany Oktoberfest
- Wimbledon
- St. Patrick's Day in Ireland!
- Pebble Beach Pro-Am
- Sundance Film Fest.
- The Iowa State Fair
- Albuquerque Balloon Fiesta
- Natl. Finals Rodeo!
- Cherry Blossom Fest.

WHEN IN ROME!
- Pray at the Vatican
- Bike Wine Country

- Surf in Oahu
- A Venice gondola ride
- Safari the Serengeti!
- Ski the Swiss Alps
- Hike Yellowstone!
- Kayak Vancouver!
- Wine-taste Tuscany
- Scuba in St. Thomas
- Cycle thru Europe
- Hockey in Montreal
- Taste pizza in that Toddlin' Town
- Hear the symphony in Boston!
- See a Broadway play!
- See a Hawaiian luau
- Raft in Jackson Hole
- Golf at St. Andrews
- Take a cable-car ride in San Francisco!

SPECIAL PLACES:
- My ancestors country
- The Smithsonian
- The Grand Canyon
- Jerusalem's Old City
- Normandy Battlefield

Travel & Enter.

95

- Stonehenge
- The Sistine Chapel
- Zion National Park
- Gettysburg!
- The Acropolis
- The Pyramids!
- Monticello
- Mount Vernon
- Niagara Falls
- Remember the Alamo!
- Go to Disneyworld!
- The Columbus Zoo
- Arlington National Cemetery
- The Grand Ole Opry

Logistics:
- Get a passport
- Be a frequent flyer
- Read books on travel
- Plan a trip every year
- Go on a road trip with my best friend

Other:
- The MLB ballparks!
- Autumn in New York
- Vermont in the Fall

- Watch a Pacific Ocean sunset
- Europe, this year!
- Hike a mountain
- Go on a golf trip
- Go on a fishing trip
- Learn to sail
- Ride a hot-air balloon
- Fly an airplane
- Visit Paris in August!
- Be part of a live TV audience in L.A.
- Plan a romantic anniversary trip!
- See China in spring
- Travel with my kids and grandkids
- Travel with my nieces and nephews
- Go down-under!
- Take Alaskan Cruise
- Schedule day trips!
- Travel with my church group
- Take a cross-country train ride!

List your Action Steps for **Travel and Entertainment:**

_____

_____

_____

_____

_____

_____

_____

_____

_____

_____

_____ **Travel & Enter.**

_____

_____

Action Steps for . . .

Time Management

- Handle papers once
- Do the least appealing tasks first!
- Make tomorrow's to-do list today
- Carry a spiral notebook at all times
- Break up large tasks/ projects into small chunks
- Start a better filing system
- Minimize interruptions
- Keep a time log
- Organize my emails in file folders
- Break the habit of multitasking
- Remain focused on activity
- Learn to say no to non-priorities
- Buy a labeler
- Eliminate unimportant tasks
- Schedule smartly

- Bookmark my top 30 websites
- Respect other people's time
- Be punctual
- Purchase easels and whiteboards
- Conquer procrastination
- Consult a time management expert
- Flag emails according to urgency
- Delegate to others
- Set up efficient work space
- Have a weekly review of tasks!
- Utilize amazing software tools
- Prioritize tasks A, B, or C
- Don't *waste* time online
- Do not hit the snooze button
- Fully complete the current task at hand!

*List your 6 to 8 Action Steps for **Time Management:***

_____

_____

_____

_____

_____

_____

_____

_____

_____

_____

_____

Action Steps for . . .

Teaching

Teaching and Coaching:
- Become a tutor
- Mentor my kids and grandkids
- Volunteer to coach
- Volunteer to teach in schools & preschools
- Volunteer at Junior Achievement
- Become a trainer
- Give cooking classes
- Teach the Bible
- Teach someone to sew or knit
- Teach kids to swim
- Teach good etiquette
- Teach kids to drive
- Teach kids to play a musical instrument
- Teach effective financial planning
- Teach survival skills
- Teach healthy eating
- Do spiritual coaching
- Do parental coaching
- Be a business coach
- Teach a continuing education class
- Perform life coaching

Writing and Presenting:
- Write that book!
- Write for magazines
- Present a class
- Begin a blog
- Start a website
- Become a facilitator
- Teach a secondary language
- Give music lessons
- Post on other's blogs
- Create a video blog
- Create interesting PowerPoint talks
- Conduct Lifelong Learning classes
- Create a podcast
- Start internet TV site
- Write others letters
- Create a workshop
- Design a training program

Other:
- Help others organize
- Pass along our family history
- Volunteer at a library

- Inspire others!
- Help others prioritize
- Start a book club
- Start a think tank
- Organize luncheons
- Become a counselor
- Be a sounding board

- Share my knowledge and experience
- Encourage others to grow
- Offer free career advice to others
- Become a team leader at work

*List your 6 to 8 Action Steps for **Teaching:***

_____

_____

_____

_____

_____

_____

_____

_____

Teaching

Action Steps for . . .

Volunteering & Philanthropy

LEARNING AND PLANNING:

- Learn more about volunteering
- Determine what will make the greatest impact
- Keep philanthropy efforts local
- Learn of *sustainable* funding strategies
- Be discernible
- Read books on giving
- Give *smartly*!
- Attend various fundraisers
- Attend a Habitat for Humanity event
- Take time to define success
- Join a philanthropic roundtable
- Find like-minded individuals

WAYS TO CONTRIBUTE:

- Host a fundraiser
- A scholarship fund!
- Set up a trust
- Volunteer my talents
- Help someone start a small business
- Donate possessions
- Create a bursary
- Give to wounded vets
- Donate to food banks and to silent auctions
- Sponsor teams
- Advertise in various event programs
- Donate to various mission causes
- Create giving circles
- Establish a charity
- Give *matching* funds
- Visit the beneficiaries
- Encourage others to participate
- Donate space, expertise & staffing!

*List Action Steps for **Volunteering and Philanthropy:***

_____

_____

_____

_____

_____

_____

_____

_____

_____

_____

_____

_____

Volunteering

Action Steps for . . .

Your 1st "Other" Category:

_____

List your Action Steps for your 1st "Other" Category:

_____

_____

_____

_____

_____

_____

_____

_____

_____

_____

_____

_____

_____

Action Steps for . . .

Your 2nd "Other" Category:

_____

List your Action Steps for your 2nd "Other" Category:

_____

_____

_____

_____

_____

_____

_____

_____

_____

_____

_____

_____

_____

Action Steps for . . .

Your 3rd "Other" Category:

_____

List your Action Steps for your 3rd "Other" Category:

_____

_____

_____

_____

_____

_____

_____

_____

_____

_____

_____

_____

_____

Chapter 8

Filling the Boxes

You're almost there! You are about 80% complete.

SINGLE PAGE LIFE PLAN

Done! *Vision Statement:* _____

_____

_____

Done! *Categories:*

Done! *Action Steps:* Now, it's time to fill the boxes:

COINS	ATTITUDES	POTHOLES	STRENGTHS

Signature _____

There are 4 boxes to your plan; *Coins, Attitudes, Potholes,* and *Strengths.*

COINS

Coins might be the coolest feature of your plan! Coins are those small things we can do every day to help make another person's life just a little better.

Coins can be viewed this way: Every day we wake up in the morning with a certain number of *Coins* in our hand that we can potentially spend.

Some days we have more *Coins* than others. For instance, if we wake up with the flu, we don't have as many *Coins* to spend. We are probably not going to shovel the snow off our neighbor's walkway, or take our nephew out to lunch.

Other days we might be filled with good health and high energy, full of creative ideas. On those days, we have our hands full of *Coins* that we can spend as we go through our day. One *Coin* might be spent calling a niece who we know could use some encouragement. Another *Coin* might be spent sending one of the 300 photographs we have of our kids, packed away in an old box on the closet floor, to our mom or dad, just to perk up their day. Or a *Coin* might be spent in the form of calling an old friend to whom we have not spoken in years.

Unfortunately, since we usually don't schedule to do these small things, time passes by and we never let people know how much we are thinking about them.

We lose our chance to do a small personal kindness for the most important people in our lives.

The problem with *Coins* is this: you either use 'em or lose 'em! Like advertising space in yesterday's newspaper, your *Coins* are a perishable item. The solution to this is to *create in advance* a list of these *Coins*. When you review your life plan, look to your *Coins* for ideas of how to strategically work small acts of thoughtfulness into your life every day!

The *Coins* you have left at the end of the day represent the unused potential of the creativity, energy, and capacity you woke up with that day. But, the good news is that you will wake up tomorrow with a whole new set of *Coins*! The more we practice using them the better we become at spending them in ways that have maximum impact.

Following are examples of *Coins* that will prompt you for ideas of *currency* you can spend.

- Mail my nephew a baseball card.
- Call my folks!
- Mail a photo from my *stack of 300*, with a note, to family and friends.
- Email an encouraging thought to a friend.
- Cut out and send a news article with note of congrats!
- Send a stamp or a coin to a young collector.

Turn page for more . . .

- Call a good friend from college.
- Thank a colleague at work.
- Compliment someone today!
- Schedule a breakfast.
- Buy someone flowers.
- Visit a sick or homebound person.
- Call a family member I haven't seen in a long time!
- Order a book online and send it to my grandfather.
- Mail to Mom that masterpiece my 3-year-old drew.
- Take my 4th-grader out of school for lunch 1 day.
- Fill up my wife's car with gas.
- Be the one to clean out the fridge!
- Subscribe to a cooking mag for the chef in my life.
- Send a box of chocolates to a friend under stress.
- Pray for someone in need.
- Tell a friend that I appreciate them.
- Shovel a neighbor's driveway.
- Bake a cake for someone's birthday.
- Skype a friend!

List 5 to 7 *Coins* that will add currency to your life:

_____

_____

_____

_____

_____

_____

_____

_____

_____

_____

_____

_____

_____

_____

Now, that's real *change*! Up next . . . *Attitudes*!

ATTITUDES

Is there really an adequate synonym for the word attitude? *Disposition, feeling, tendency* all seem to fall short.

There are bad attitudes, good attitudes, positive and negative attitudes.

We refer to self-defeating attitudes and goal-achieving attitudes. We can take a complacent attitude towards things, while at other times our attitudes are considered deep-seeded.

Attitudes can seem intangible, but they lead to powerful and tangible results. They leverage our efforts.

Attitudes fortify over time, the more we use them.

Most importantly, attitudes are not forced upon us. We *choose* our attitude. We *take* on an attitude. We *adopt* an attitude.

Now is the time for you to adopt with intentionality those attitudes that will best help you live your *Single Page Life Plan* on a daily basis.

Choose 5 *Attitudes* that resonate with your life plan from the following two pages.

Attitudes

- You cannot be grateful and sad at the same time!
- Attitude is as important as ability.
- I have an attitude of gratitude!
- Be happy, cheerful, positive, and optimistic!
- Courage is granted to the prepared!
- Be confident of myself and respectful of others.
- Carpe Diem! Seize the Day!
- I will persevere, I will endure, I will succeed!
- I have an open and accepting attitude.
- We can't change the past; we change the future!
- The harder I work, the more fortunate I become.
- Keep a loving and compassionate attitude.
- When one door closes, another one opens.
- Being rich or poor is simply a frame of mind.
- I have a conscientious and considerate attitude.
- I am a warrior and a protector.
- Keep a humble and unpretentious attitude.
- Have a tolerant, accepting, and inclusive attitude.
- Leadership is earned. Earn it every day!
- The best leadership is leading by example.
- A cheerful heart is good medicine.

Turn page for more . . .

o Happiness and contentment is an attitude.

o Good attitudes lead to good actions & a good life.

o Keep a playful and humorous attitude.

o Love is patient and kind. Love never ends.

o I ultimately succeed by helping others achieve.

o I take on, choose, and adopt my own attitudes.

o "So do not worry about tomorrow; for tomorrow will take care of itself." [Matthew 6:34]

o We all fall. How we get up is what matters most!

o "99% of the failures come from people who have the habit of making excuses." – George Washington

o "Happiness depends more upon the internal frame of a person's own mind, than on the external in the world." – George Washington

o "The future does not belong to the fainthearted; it belongs to the brave." – Ronald Reagan

o "We have every right to dream heroic dreams." – Ronald Reagan

o "Happiness ... lies in the joy of achievement, in the thrill of creative effort." – Franklin D. Roosevelt

o "Happiness depends on ourselves." – Aristotle

On the following page, list the *Attitudes* you want to adopt in your life ...

These are 5 *Attitudes* that I choose to adopt:

_____

_____

_____

_____

_____

_____

_____

_____

_____

_____

_____

_____

_____

_____

Watch Your Step!

POTHOLES

Potholes are those things to avoid. They are the distractions to your plan; landmines! Here you have to dig deep to find those things that signify a real threat to your life plan.

For instance, if you spend an hour each day playing computer-euchre on the Internet, it's probably a good guess that computer-euchre hasn't yet earned its way to your page one! If you put it in the *Potholes box*, that single hour each day will save you the equivalent of 9 forty-hour work weeks every year!

Think about that! Just by eliminating 1 hour each day of unproductive activity, you gain 9 forty-hour work weeks. This illustrates the incredible power that comes with adding intentionality to your life.

On the next page, are some examples of *Potholes* you might want to avoid. Use this list for ideas of *Potholes* that might be tripping you up. Circle a few, and then cross out all but 5 of them.

Potholes

- ○ Hanging out with negative people
- ○ Fearing change
- ○ Being late for meetings
- ○ Watching too much television
- ○ Dating incompatible people
- ○ Living on Facebook!
- ○ Over-consuming food and drink
- ○ Getting too little sleep
- ○ Shopping too much
- ○ Talking too much on the phone
- ○ Over-committing my time
- ○ Surfing for hours on the internet
- ○ Drinking and partying
- ○ Holding onto the past
- ○ Long-distance relationships
- ○ Trying to make things perfect
- ○ Arguing with people
- ○ Reading too many newspapers
- ○ Obsessing on fashion
- ○ Watching too much *sports*!
- ○ Following the pack
- ○ Being too sensitive to criticism
- ○ Staying up too late at night
- ○ Not asking for help

Turn page for more . . .

o Idleness

o Eating past 7:00 p.m.

o Work flings

o Obsessing on politics

o Taking things for granted

o Unwarranted worry

o Not facing problems head-on

o Over-Tweeting and Over-Pinteresting

o Irrational self-doubt

o Clutter!

o Procrastination

o Fear of making mistakes!

These are 5 *Potholes* I want to avoid:

_____

_____

_____

_____

_____

_____

_____

_____

_____

STRENGTHS

Strengths are those things that we don't often consider. But, you must identify those character attributes that make you special; those talents you can draw upon to help others. You must identify those qualifications that help you make a positive impact everywhere you go.

Your *Single Page Life Plan* requires that you maintain a R.A.P. sheet.

○ **R**ecognize all of your strengths, skills, and assets. False modesty is not permitted here! What is your unique genius?

○ **A**ssess which of these specifically pertain to you accomplishing the Action Steps of your life plan.

○ **P**ut them to work! Review this box to remind yourself to implement those unique qualities that will help turn your dreams into reality!

Review the *Strengths* on the following page to help you determine your unique abilities and attributes.

Strengths

Circle several of the examples of *Strengths*, and then cross out all but 7. Use this list to brainstorm.

- o I am a quick learner
- o I have a good sense of humor
- o I am a good teacher
- o I know how to motivate others
- o I am a good planner
- o I am very good at languages
- o I have good presentation and speaking skills
- o I am very organized
- o I am physically strong
- o I can stay focused on things
- o I find the humor in life
- o I understand social media
- o Coaching comes easy to me
- o Others can rely on me
- o My reputation in the industry is good
- o I always give 100%!
- o I am able to accept reasonable risk
- o I enjoy leading!
- o My financial and accounting skill are outstanding!
- o I am honest

○ I have an energetic attitude

○ I keep a positive attitude

○ I am musically inclined

○ I am very friendly to others

○ I have a lot of experience and wisdom

○ I am athletic

○ I have been blessed with good health

○ I am artistically talented

○ I am very a prayerful person

○ I am both creative and logical

○ I am good under pressure

○ I am a trustworthy person

○ I have a natural ability to cook

○ I am a good writer

○ My capacity to work hard is high

○ I am very creative

○ I am mechanically inclined

○ I am a resilient person

○ I have a pleasant personality

○ I am well-educated

○ I have a phenomenal memory

○ I am highly motivated

○ I am intuitive

○ I can dance!

Turn page for more . . .

○ I am well-read and well-informed

○ I negotiate well

○ My selling skills are very strong

○ I enjoy what I do

○ My leadership skills are strong

List 7 of your significant *Strengths* that will most help you achieve your *Single Page Life Plan*:

_____

_____

_____

_____

_____

_____

_____

_____

_____

_____

_____

_____

_____

_____

Chapter 9

Creating
Single Page Checklists

Once you experience the benefits of the *Single Page* format, you will see that it brings the same concise focus and workability to your other unique projects. The *Single Page* strategy can be used for your special projects, wedding plans, vacation getaways, social media initiatives, personal fitness goals, branding campaigns, college searches, training programs, company holiday parties, new sales promotions, customer satisfaction policies, etc.

Let's use event planning as an example. Since most of us are familiar with the many different things that are involved with orchestrating a wedding, and the reception that follows, let's see how this could be reduced to a *Single Page Checklist*.

Before you do this, however, you might want to remember the advice my wife and I received, a week before our own wedding. We were told, *Remember… It's all about the marriage, not the wedding!* That is a difficult thing to keep in mind when you are about to have a couple hundred people show up to see the two of you exchange vows, but how true it is!

At **www.SinglePageLifePlan.com** you will find similar *Single Page Checklists* for other types of projects related to personal fitness, social media marketing, business checklists, etc.

Turn the page to see a *Single Page Wedding Checklist* that an engaged couple might create for their big day!

Wedding Plan Checklist ...

SINGLE PAGE
CHECKLIST: *WEDDING PLAN*

IMPORTANT DATES	CEREMONY	ATTIRE
_____ Wedding Day	VOWS	DETERMINE OUR BUDGET
_____ Meeting w/ Clergy/Officiant	BRIDESMAIDS SELECTION	WEDDING GOWN & VEIL
_____ Wedding Rehearsal	GROOMS SELECTION	BRIDESMAID DRESSES
_____ Rehearsal Dinner	READERS	SEVERAL FITTINGS
_____ Wedding Reception	FLOWER GIRL	SHOES
_____ Bridesmaid Luncheon	CEREMONY PAMPHLETS	BOUQUETS/CORSAGES
_____ Order Bridesmaid Dresses	PHOTOGRAPHER	PARENTS OF THE COUPLE
_____ Order Tuxedos	VIDEOGRAPHER	GROOMS ATTIRE
_____ Mailing of Invitations	VENUE	REHEARSAL ATTIRE
_____ Wedding Day Hair Appt.	OFFICIANT	CHANGE OF CLOTHES FOR THE RECEPTION
_____ Room Reservations for Out of Town Guests	FLORIST ARRANGEMENT	PRESSING & STEAMING
_____ Room Reservations for Bride and Groom	MUSIC AND/OR SINGERS	READERS ATTIRE
_____ Honeymoon!	MARRIAGE LICENSE	FLOWER GIRL & OTHERS
	RINGS	

THINGS TO REMEMBER!	GET ME THERE ON TIME!	IT'S ALL IN THE DETAILS!
REGISTER WITH GIFT REGISTER	SCHEDULE THE LIMO AND ARRANGE TRANSPORT FOR ALL OUT OF TOWN GUESTS	REMIND EVERYONE OF TIMES
SELECT ATTENDANT GIFTS		LAST MINUTE CONTACT SHEET
GROOMS & BRIDESMAIDS GIFTS	TRANSPORT FOR BRIDAL PARTY & PARENTS & GRANDPARENTS TO & FROM REHEARSAL DINNER	GUEST BOOKS AND BUBBLES!
MAID OF HONOR GIFT		MANICURES & PEDICURES
OFFICIANT GIFT	PRE-PROGRAM GPS DEVICES	WRAP GIFTS & NOTIFY PAPERS
RING BEARER GIFT	MAKE SURE GAS IS TOPPED OFF	LOOK FOR LEFT BEHIND ITEMS

GUEST LIST & MAILING

DETERMINE HER LIST

DETERMINE HIS LIST

RECEPTION SEATING

SELECT INVITATIONS

GET THANK YOU NOTES AND ANNOUNCEMENTS

REHEARSAL DINNER LIST

PERSONAL STATIONARY

SELECT MAILING STAMPS

PHONE LIST OF EVERY PERSON & COMPANY INVOLVED W/ WEDDING

SEND OUT WEDDING ANNOUNCMENT TO PAPER AFTER WEDDING

SEND OUT THANK YOU NOTES TO GIFT-GIVERS

PHOTOGRAPHER/MUSIC

PICK A PHOTOGRAPHER

PICK A VIDEOGRAPHER

CHOOSE A DISC JOCKEY AND/OR A BAND

MUSIC ARRANGEMENT

DECIDE ON SELECTIONS

SINGER FOR CEREMONY

VIOLIN FOR REHEARSAL?

BRIDAL PORTAIT SETTING

DECIDE WHEN THE PHOTOS WILL BE TAKEN

DISPOSABLE CAMERAS AT RECEPTION TABLES?

RECORD VARIOUS TOASTS AT RECEPTION?

RECEPTION

DECIDE ON A LOCATION

MEET WITH A PLANNER

SELECT MENU FOR FOOD

REFRESHMENTS

SELECT A CATERER

ORDER A WEDDING CAKE

CHOOSE ARRANGMENTS AND FLOWERS FOR THE TABLES AT RECEPTION

GO OVER DETAILS WITH CATERERS AND HOTEL MANAGERS

MAKE A SEATING LIST

RESERVE ARCHES AND FLORAL PILLARS

HAVE A ROOM FOR GIFTS

IT'S ALL ABOUT THE MARRIAGE

SHOW GRATITUDE TO ALL!

ENJOY THE MOMENT

BE ACCOMODATING

BE LOVING TO MY SPOUSE

DON'T EXPECT PERFECTION

DON'T FRET THE SMALL STUFF!

HONEYMOON

WHERE DO WE GO? HOW LONG?

GET PLANE TICKETS AND MAKE ALL HOTEL RESERVATIONS

PASSPORTS & IDENTIFICATION & ANY NEEDED INNOCULATIONS

PRE PACK

GET A RIDE TO THE AIRPORT!

Chapter 10

You Have Your Work
Cut Out for You

The phrase, *You have your work cut out for you,* dates back over 400 years and occurs in *A Christmas Carol* by Charles Dickens. It is thought to have originated with tailors who would cut out a pattern of a suit or a dress. It was their way of preparing everything in an organized fashion before stitching it all together.

Now is the time for you to stitch together the design you have chosen for your *Single Page Life Plan.*

Following is how to piece together the 5 elements of your plan:

FIRST

Transfer the *Vision Statement*, *Life Categories*, *Action Steps*, and *Boxes* onto a piece of paper that is roughly the same size as the template provided at the back of this book. This will help you scale the words you are writing to fit inside the respective areas of your life plan.

NEXT

Transfer the rough draft onto the provided template. Remember, this is not supposed to be (or look perfect). It is supposed to be used!

FINALLY

You will want to make several copies of your plan. While *Single Page Life Plan* is copyright protected and cannot be reproduced for commercial or business use, you may make several copies of your plan for your own personal use. Place copies at work and home; wherever you will most likely have time to review, change, and update your plan.

Chapter 11

Your Signature Here, Please!

SIGN IT!

To do something on purpose is to do something with a desired outcome; to do something with a planned consequence! By signing your life plan, you are making a promise to yourself that you will live your life on purpose.

You are challenging yourself to follow a strategic set of *Action Steps* for every important category of your life to help you achieve the vision you have for your future.

MAKE COPIES!

Keep one copy in this book. Keep other copies at work, at home, and wherever else you are most likely to often see them.

WORK IT!

Review it, change it, highlight it, scratch it up with a pencil, and throw it away when you feel it's time to create a new one. But, always *work* it!

REMEMBER:

Don't try to make your plan perfect, or you'll *never* get it done!

Peripheries are not priorities. Don't overload your life plan.

Your *Single Page Life Plan* must be continually updated; not set in stone.

Don't be shy—share your plans with others. Stay accountable!

Life Categories and *Action Steps* must *earn* their way to page one!

The *Action Steps* turn your life's vision into reality.

Simplify complexity! Do as Einstein did; chop away all of the clutter!

Be a magnifying glass! Don't allow your energy to be diffused. Focus your energy on the truly significant.

You get a fresh set of *Coins* daily. Spend wisely!

Synchronize everything to your *Vision Statement*.

Watch out for *Potholes*. Saving just one hour per day creates the equivalent of 9 work weeks every year!

Assess your personal *Strengths*. There is only 1 you!

Finally, thank you for taking your valuable time to read this book. I hope that it results in a life plan that is truly life-changing. If you find time to share the impact it makes on your life, please visit www. SinglePageLifePlan.com and tell us your story!

I am so pleased to have written this book for you . . . it was on my life plan!

Sincerely,

Garrett K. Scanlon

About the Author

GARRETT K. SCANLON works with leaders who want to give their colleagues a unique tool for achieving greater purpose and higher energy throughout the day. That tool is a *Single Page Life Plan* that helps them become more intentional, better organized, and happier at work and home.

Garrett's career began as an expert in investment real estate where he has represented clients in the sale and purchase of over $400 million of investment property, and served as Director of Sales and Leasing for CASTO, one of the oldest and largest family-owned development companies of retail shopping centers in the United States.

Since 2005, Garrett has been sharing with his audiences real life stories from his experiences in the marketplace. He has authored several books including *Walking and Talking: 57 Stories of Success and Humor in the Real Estate World of Business*, *Lifeboard: How to Form Your Own Personal Board of Directors*, and a book for young adults, *Seeing Past Friday Night*.

Everyone who attends a life-planning seminar or training session by Garrett, receives a personalized *Single Page Life Plan*, a simple, yet life-changing *takeaway* that adds purpose and energy to their day.

Garrett Scanlon, and his wife, Sherri, live in Columbus, Ohio.

To bring Garrett into your company, group, or school please visit his website:

www.SinglePageLifePlan.com

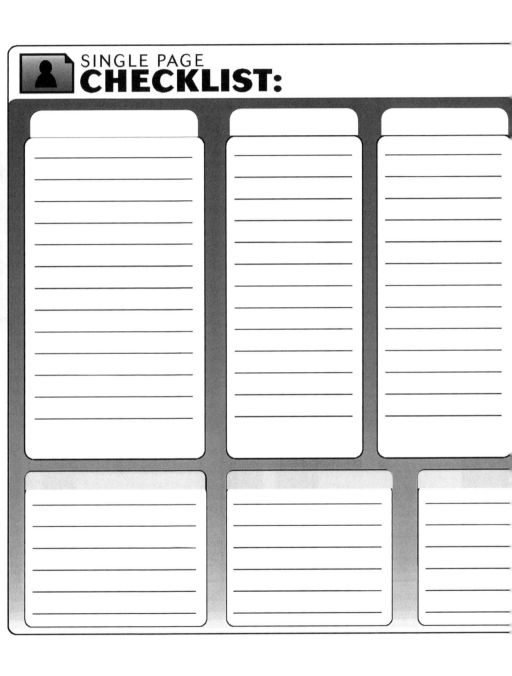

SINGLE PAGE
CHECKLIST: